Aboriginal Canadian Communities
CREE COMMUNITY

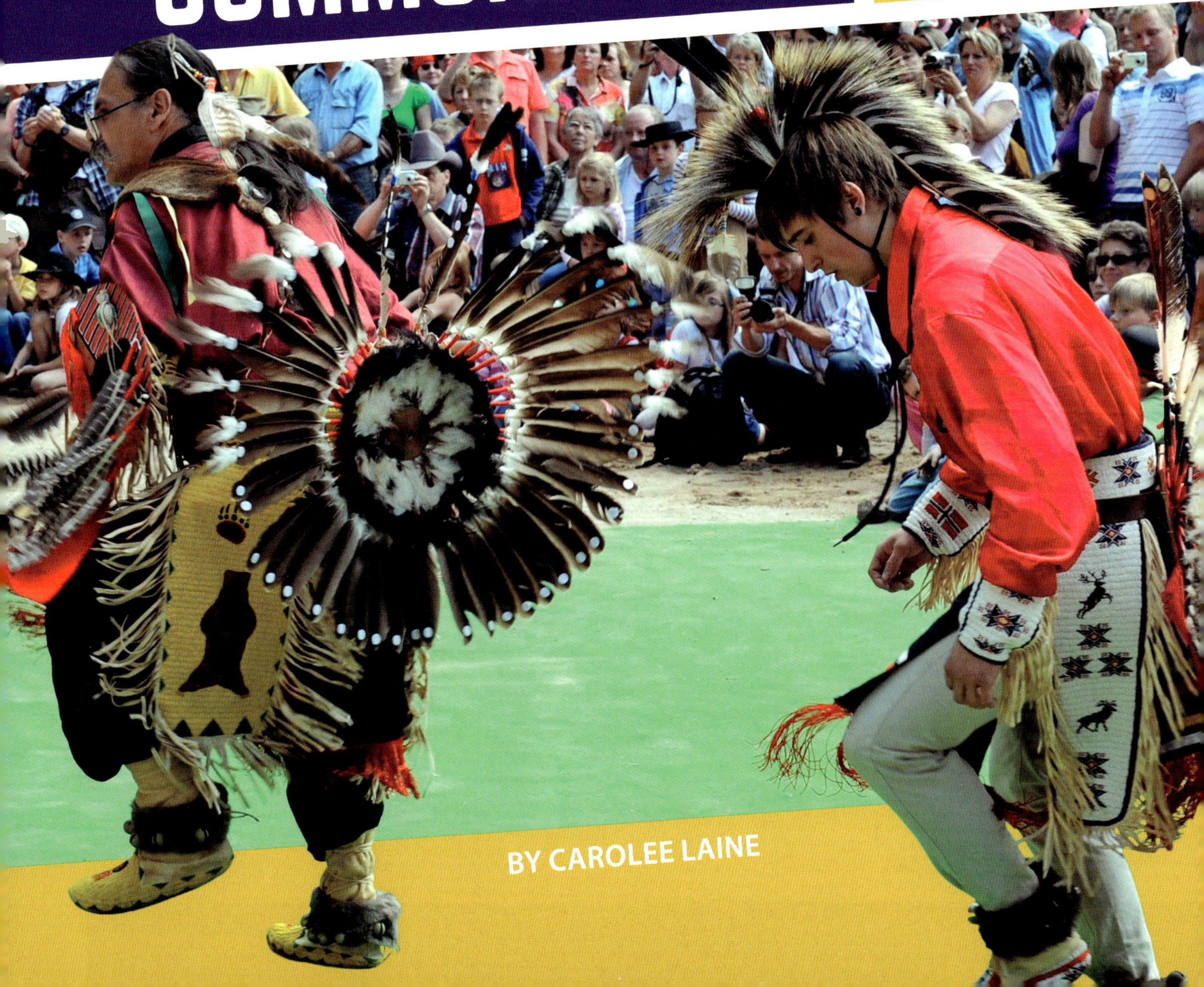

BY CAROLEE LAINE

True North is published by Beech Street Books
27 Stewart Rd. Collingwood, ON Canada L9Y 4M7

Copyright © 2017 by Beech Street Books. All rights reserved. No part of this book may be reproduced or utilized in any form or by any means without written permission from the publisher.

www.beechstreetbooks.ca

Produced by Red Line Editorial

Photographs ©: Matthias Hiekel/EPACorbis, cover, 1; Nikki Carlson/Havre Daily News/AP Images, 4–5, 16–17; Ryan Remiorz/The Canadian Press/AP Images, 6; Megapress/Alamy, 8–9; Charles Horetzky/Bibliothèque et Archives Canada/C-005181, 10; Library and Archives Canada/C-008183, 12–13; Bud Glunz/National Film Board of Canada/Photothèque/PA-134110, 15; Kevin Frayer/AP Images, 18; Fred Chartrand/The Canadian Press/AP Images, 20; Red Line Editorial, 21

Editor: Amanda Lanser
Designer: Laura Polzin
Content Consultant: Dr. Ronald Niezen, Associate Professor of Anthropology and Canada Research Chair in the Comparative Study of Indigenous Rights and Identity, McGill University

Library and Archives Canada Cataloguing in Publication

Laine, Carolee, author
    Cree community / by Carolee Laine.

(Aboriginal Canadian communities)
Includes bibliographical references and index.
Issued in print and electronic formats.
ISBN 978-1-77308-000-0 (hardback).--ISBN 978-1-77308-028-4 (paperback).--
ISBN 978-1-77308-056-7 (pdf).--ISBN 978-1-77308-084-0 (html)

    1. Cree Indians--Juvenile literature. 2. Cree Indians--Social life and customs--Juvenile literature. 3. Cree Indians--History--Juvenile literature. I. Title.

E99.C88L36 2016   j971.004'97323   C2016-903116-0
                                                                         C2016-903117-9

Printed in the United States of America
Mankato, MN
August 2016

TABLE OF CONTENTS

WHO ARE THE CREE? 4

DAILY LIFE IN A CREE COMMUNITY 8

OLD WAYS AND NEW WAYS 12

CELEBRATING CREE LIFE 16

Map 20
Glossary 22
To Learn More 23
Index/About the Author 24

Chapter One

WHO ARE THE CREE?

First Nations are the people who first lived in the area that is now Canada. Cree people are the largest group of First Nations who share a language. There are five major Cree language groups: Western/Plains Cree, Northern/Woodland Cree, Central/Swampy Cree, Moose Cree, and Eastern Cree. Within these groups, there are hundreds of Cree communities. They have different cultures and **traditions**. The name *Cree* is a short form of the French word *Kristeneaux*. In their own language, the Plains Cree call themselves *Nehiyawak*. It means "the people." In Eastern and Moose Cree, the term is Eeyou.

LIFE YESTERDAY AND TODAY

Early Cree territory spanned from modern-day Quebec through Alberta. Cree ways of life depended on where

Cree students perform traditional dances.

SAY IT

tânisi (tahn-see): hello, how are you?

Plains Cree from Saskatchewan work to protect their land rights.

communities lived. Woodland Cree lived in forests. They were hunters, trappers, and gatherers who moved with the seasons. They paddled **canoes** along waterways in summer. They wore **snowshoes** to get around in winter.

Plains Cree lived on the prairies in western North America. They rode horses and hunted bison. They moved with the bison herds. Plains Cree hunters used bows and arrows until the **fur trade** introduced them to rifles. Plains Cree traded bison meat to fur trappers and traders.

Today, some Cree people live on reserves. Reserves are lands the government set aside just for First Nations. But many Cree people also live in cities and other communities in Canada. Modern Cree live in houses or apartments. They ride buses or drive cars to work or school. Many Cree use snowmobiles to get around in winter. Some speak their Cree language. But most also speak English or French.

CONTINUING TRADITIONS

Protecting Earth's land, water, plants, and animals has always been important to Cree communities. Cree people believe all living things must be treated with respect. In the past, everything they needed came from the land. They hunted animals and fished. They gathered plants for food and medicines. Modern Cree continue to use and respect the land. The Canadian government and large companies sometimes want to use Cree lands for other reasons. Cree lands have been used for logging, mining, and to make electricity. The Cree people work to protect the land and their rights to continue using it.

Cree people use stories to share their history. Other stories explain Cree ways of life or Cree laws. The stories are about humans, animals, spirits, and mystical events. In some Cree schools, children learn how the Cree lived hundreds of years ago. They learn stories that have been passed down for many years. In daily life today, many Cree people practise the activities their ancestors did. They celebrate the history of their people.

Chapter Two

DAILY LIFE IN A CREE COMMUNITY

Woodland Cree lived in villages in the summertime. The villages broke up into small groups of families in wintertime. The groups hunted, fished, and trapped together. Men and women shared community duties. Women bent branches into dome-shaped wigwams. They covered these homes with birch bark or animal skins. In winter, they built wooden lodges insulated with moss. Men hunted large animals, such as caribou and moose. Women hunted small animals close to their villages. Entire communities fished and gathered wild berries and other plants.

Women made clothing from animal skins. They wore long dresses. Men wore long shirts and leggings. In winter, both men

In wintertime, Cree lived together in small family groups.

SAY IT

paskwâwimostos (pa-skwow-ih-mus-tus): Plains bison

A Plains Cree teepee camp on the Alberta prairie

and women wore warm robes made of animal fur. Women used beads, feathers, and **quills** to decorate their clothing.

Children helped their parents and **elders**. This is how they learned to look after themselves. They learned to trap small animals, gather plants, make clothing, and cook. They learned how to make canoes.

EARLY PLAINS CREE

Plains Cree also did not live in one place. They followed the bison herds. They set up movable **teepee** camps. Plains Cree built cone-shaped teepees with tree

poles covered by bison skins. Though heavy, the teepees could be taken down. Plains Cree could take their homes with them. Cree hunters rode horses to hunt bison. Horses could travel farther and faster than people on foot. Hunters used bows and arrows or guns to shoot bison. These large animals provided food, clothing, and shelter for a whole community. Nothing was wasted.

Women cut strips of bison meat to dry in the sun. They made **pemmican**, a food that lasted a long time. Women used bison hides to cover teepees and make clothing. They made tools from bison bones and hair. Plains Cree children learned these tasks from adults. They learned to be thankful for the animals that helped their people live on the plains.

CREE COMMUNITIES TODAY

Today, many Cree live in cities and towns, but some live on reserves. Cree reserves have government leaders called chiefs. Reserve residents elect their chiefs. Cree people living outside the reserve can vote, too. Cree people preserve the old ways of life. They speak English or French. But they also learn the Cree language. They learn traditional and modern songs, dances, and arts.

Modern Cree children go to school and learn the same subjects as other children. Some reserves run schools for Cree children. Students learn about Cree cultures. Children learn to respect nature and value the history of their people. Many Canadian public schools are starting to teach the histories and cultures of the Cree people, too.

Chapter Three

OLD WAYS AND NEW WAYS

Cree people have lived in North America for thousands of years. But 500 years ago, French explorers and English fur traders arrived in Cree territory. Contact with Europeans changed the Cree way of life.

THE FUR TRADE

Woodland and Swampy Cree people were skilled animal trappers. Animal fur was very popular in Europe in the 1500s. European fur traders built **trading posts** in Cree territory. They offered Cree communities European goods, such as metal pots, knives, cloth, and guns. In exchange, the Cree traded their furs. Cree communities valued their relationships with European fur traders. The new tools saved them time and effort. Cree trappers

Cree trappers traded animal furs for valuable goods.

spent more time hunting animals for fur. If they met European demand for furs, they could meet their own demands for European goods.

NEW DISEASES

Not all contact with Europeans helped the Cree. Increased contact with Europeans spread new illnesses. Europeans had **immunity** from these European diseases. But the Cree could not fight off these illnesses. One disease was called smallpox. Nearly all Cree who caught smallpox died from it.

HARMFUL NEW LAWS

Between 1871 and 1921, the Canadian government signed 11 **treaties** with First Nations communities. Together, they are called the Numbered Treaties. The treaties outlined benefits and responsibilities between these nations. But First Nations and the Canadian government interpreted the treaties differently. First Nations communities believed the treaties outlined how lands were shared. The Canadian government believed they gave Canada the right to First Nations land.

Cree leaders were wary of signing a treaty. They had witnessed other treaties take away land from other First Nations groups. But in 1876, the Cree people were facing starvation. The leaders agreed to share Cree land with the government. In exchange, Plains and Woodland Cree would get help with farming.

In 1876, the Canadian government passed the Indian Act. It ignored past treaties. Cree and other Aboriginal children were sent away to live in

Cree children sit in their classroom at a Saskatchewan residential school.

residential schools. They were forced to learn European ways of life. Children were not allowed to speak their own languages. Wearing traditional clothing was banned. The children could not visit their families.

FIGHTING FOR TREATY RIGHTS

The Numbered Treaties and Indian Act have affected Cree communities for nearly 150 years. They are still in effect today. In the 1800s, many Cree argued their old ways of life were disappearing. They felt the government was treating them unfairly. Since then, Cree leaders have fought for the rights of their communities. They negotiate new treaties and agreements with the Canadian government. Some give communities more control of their lands and natural resources. Others expand the ability of Cree leaders to govern their communities.

Chapter Four

CELEBRATING CREE LIFE

Cree communities pass down skills, songs, dances, and art. These traditions have been part of Cree life for hundreds of years. Cree communities continue to celebrate these traditions today.

WALKING-OUT CEREMONY

The Walking-Out Ceremony is an important Cree celebration. It is for children who have just learned to walk. It welcomes the children into their community. It recognizes each child's value as a member of society.

The children dress in traditional clothes. Adults give them toy versions of Cree tools. Elders await the children in a ceremonial tent. The elders give the children hunted animals that have been decorated. Then, the children walk out of the tent. They take

A Cree drum group leads students in a Round Dance.

SAY IT

nĩmihito (nay-mih-tuh): to dance

A Cree girl celebrates National Aboriginal Day in 2011.

their first steps in their community. They pull the animals behind them. The children walk around a small tree. Halfway around, they pretend to use their toy tools. After completing the circle, they return to the elders. They give the elders the animals they were pulling.

HONOURING WISDOM AND TRADITIONS

The Cree also honour the elders in their communities. At gatherings, elders have the best seats and eat first. Cree respect elders for their wisdom and experience. Elders teach their communities about traditional ways of life.

On June 21 each year, Cree and other First Nations gather in communities across Canada. They celebrate National Aboriginal Day. They honour old ways of life with dances, songs, stories, games, and feasts. They celebrate the achievements of First Nations communities.

MUSIC AND ART

Music and dancing are important parts of Cree celebrations. Some dances, such as the Sun Dance, are part of Cree spiritual beliefs. Dancers wear special clothing decorated with beads and colourful feathers. It takes craftspeople many months to make them. They sometimes wear bells around their ankles. The bells jingle as they dance. Cree perform these dances for special occasions.

Cree artists make beautiful paintings and beadwork. These skills have been passed down for many years. They create art to sell and spread knowledge of Cree cultures. They want young Cree people to be proud of their heritage.

> **INQUIRY QUESTIONS**
>
> Why did students have to attend residential schools? How would you feel if you were forced to leave your family and learn a new language and new customs?

CREE TERRITORY

Historic Cree territory reached from modern-day Quebec west beyond modern-day Alberta. Communities of Eastern Cree, Moose Cree, and Swampy Cree lived east and south of Hudson Bay. Swampy Cree territory extended west across modern-day Ontario and Manitoba. Woodland Cree lived in Manitoba, Saskatchewan, and Alberta. Plains Cree lived west and south of these communities.

Today, Cree reserves are found across historical Cree territory and beyond. Most are located in Manitoba, Saskatchewan, and Alberta. Some reserves are also located along the shore of Hudson Bay and in Quebec.

Members of the James Bay Cree community participate in a rally on Parliament Hill in Ottawa.

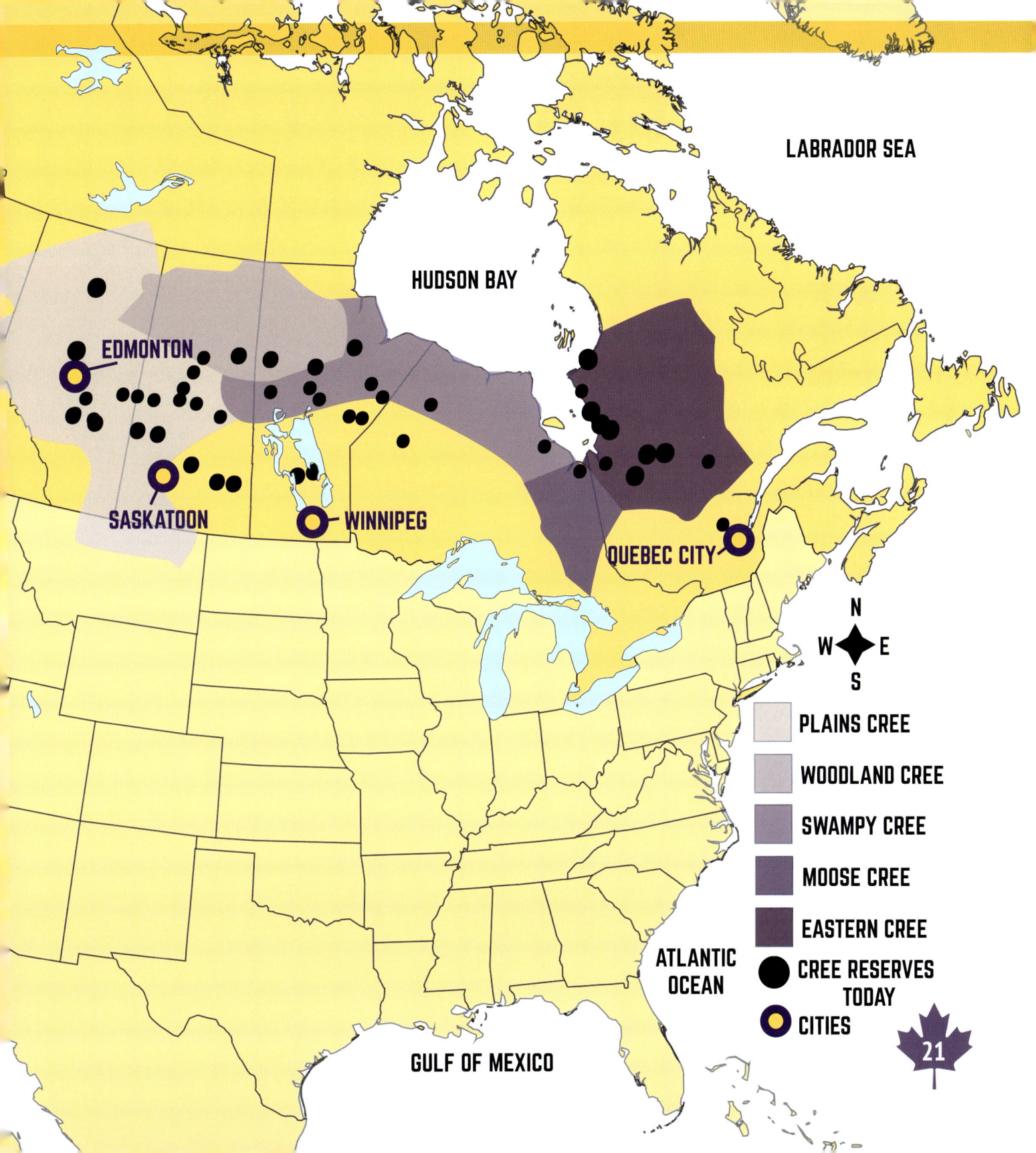

GLOSSARY

CANOES
long, narrow boats moved with paddles

ELDERS
people whom the community respects as leaders in teaching cultural values

FUR TRADE
business in which people traded goods for beaver and other fur

IMMUNITY
ability to resist a disease

PEMMICAN
dried meat mixed with melted fat and berries

QUILLS
sharp spines on a porcupine's back

SNOWSHOES
wide frames that attach to a person's feet to help them walk on top of snow without sinking

TEEPEE
a cone-shaped tent that was used as a home by some Aboriginal Canadian communities

TRADING POSTS
places where people exchange goods

TRADITIONS
beliefs and customs passed on from one generation to another

TREATIES
agreements between groups made through negotiation

TO LEARN MORE

BOOKS

Banting, Erinn. *Cree*. Calgary: Weigl, 2008.

Goldsworthy, Kaite. *Saskatchewan*. Calgary: Weigl, 2014.

Gurtler, Janet. *Teepees*. Calgary: Weigl, 2013.

WEBSITES

Plains Cree
Library and Archives Canada
https://www.collectionscanada.gc.ca/settlement/kids/021013-2161-e.html

SICC Animation Project for Youth
Saskatchewan Indian Cultural Centre
http://www.sicc.sk.ca/sicc-animation-project-for-youth.html

Terminology and Usage
University of Ottawa
http://www.med.uottawa.ca/sim/data/Aboriginal_Intro_e.htm

INDEX

bison, 6–7, 10–11

celebrations, 7, 16, 18–19
ceremonies, 16–18
children, 7, 8–10, 11, 14–15, 16–18

daily life, 8–11

Eastern Cree, 4, 20
education, 7, 9–10, 11, 14–15
elders, 8, 16–18

fur trade, 7, 12–14

illnesses, 14

languages, 4, 7, 11, 15

Moose Cree, 4, 20

Plains Cree, 4, 6, 10–11, 20

reserves, 7, 11, 20

spiritual beliefs, 7, 19
Sun Dance, 19
Swampy Cree, 4, 12, 20

teepees, 10, 11
treaties, 14–15

Walking-Out Ceremony, 16–18
wigwams, 8
Woodland Cree, 4, 6, 8–10, 12, 14, 20

ABOUT THE AUTHOR

Carolee Laine is an educator and children's writer. She has written social studies textbooks and other educational materials. She enjoys researching and writing non-fiction books for young readers.